'60s GUITAR RIFFS

ISBN-13: 978-0-634-00163-5
ISBN-10: 0-634-00163-9

HAL•LEONARD® CORPORATION

7777 W. BLUEMOUND RD. P.O. BOX 13819 MILWAUKEE, WI 53213

Visit Hal Leonard Online at
www.halleonard.com

CONTENTS

All Along the Watchtower

Words and Music by Bob Dylan

Tune down 1/2 step:
(low to high) Eb–Ab–Db–Gb–Bb–Eb

Intro

Moderately ♩ = 112

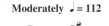

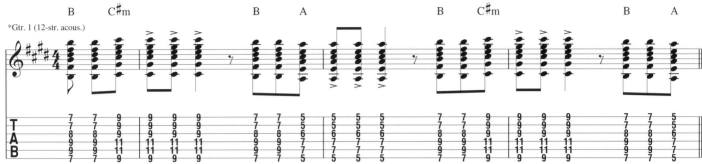

*Gtr. 1 (12-str. acous.)

*Two gtrs. arr. for one.

Artist: Jimi Hendrix Experience
Album: *Electric Ladyland*
Year: 1968
Guitarists: Jimi Hendrix, Dave Mason (12-string)

Trivia: Hendrix recorded the bass guitar for this track (his only U.S. Top 40 single ever released) because Experience bassist Noel Redding had gone out for a beer and Hendrix wanted the recording process to move along faster.

All Day and All of the Night

Words and Music by Ray Davies

Intro

Gtr. 1
(dist.)

Moderate Rock ♩ = 138

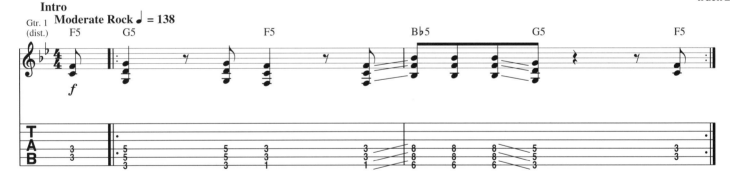

Artist: The Kinks
Album: *Kinks-Size*
Year: 1964
Guitarists: Ray Davies, Dave Davies

Trivia: Kinks guitarist Ray Davies successfully sued The Doors because their 1968 single "Hello, I Love You" is musically almost identical to this #7 hit.

Birthday

Words and Music by John Lennon and Paul McCartney

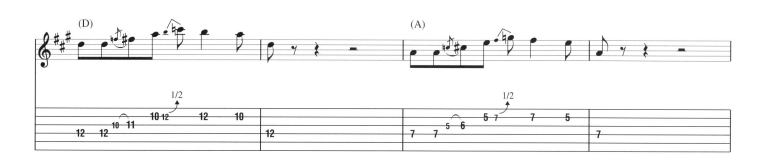

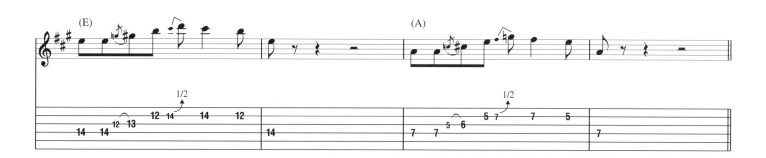

Artist: The Beatles **Album:** *The Beatles* **Year:** 1968 **Guitarists:** John Lennon, George Harrison	**Trivia:** Yoko Ono, Linda Eastman (McCartney), and Pattie Boyd-Harrison contributed backing vocals to this track, singing the word "birthday."

Born to Be Wild

Words and Music by Mars Bonfire

Track 4

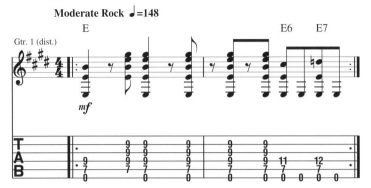

Artist: Steppenwolf

Album: *Steppenwolf*

Year: 1968

Guitarists: John Kay, Michael Monarch

Trivia: This #2 hit, which may have inspired the genre name "heavy metal," has been covered by hard-hitters such as Slayer, The Cult, Slade, Blue Öyster Cult, and Ozzy Osbourne. The latter curiously is a duet with Miss Piggy of the Muppets.

Gloria

Words and Music by Van Morrison

Track 7

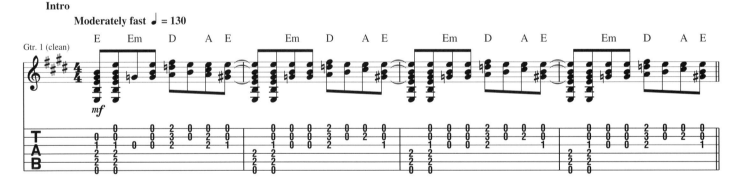

Artist: Shadows of Knight

Album: *Gloria*

Year: 1966

Guitarists: Joe Kelley, Jerry McGeorge

Trivia: This song has been covered numerous times by artists such as John Lee Hooker (featuring songwriter Van Morrison), The Doors, David Bowie, the Rolling Stones, Jimi Hendrix, the Grateful Dead and R.E.M. Perhaps this is due to the fact that it isn't difficult to learn, as humorist Dave Barry has joked that "if you throw a guitar on the ground, it will all by itself play 'Gloria'."

California Dreamin'

Words and Music by John Phillips and Michelle Phillips

Artist: The Mamas & The Papas

Album: *If You Can Believe Your Eyes and Ears*

Year: 1966

Guitarist: John Phillips

Trivia: Singer Barry McGuire, who introduced The Mamas & The Papas to the head of Dunhill Records, recorded this song for his 1966 album *This Precious Time* with The Mamas & The Papas singing background vocals.

Fortunate Son

Words and Music by John Fogerty

Tune down 1 step:
(low to high) D–G–C–F–A–D

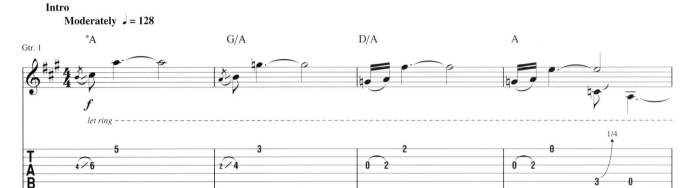

*Chord symbols reflect overall harmony.

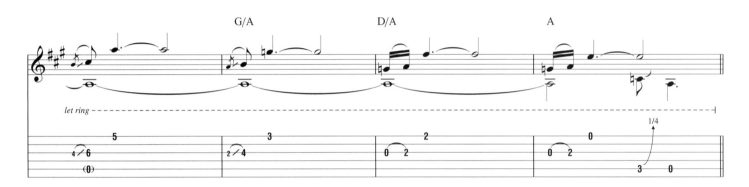

Artist: Creedence Clearwater Revival
Album: *Willy and the Poor Boys*
Year: 1969
Guitarists: John Fogerty, Tom Fogerty

Trivia: Though rumor has stated that John Fogerty may have had Vice President Al Gore, Jr. (whose father was also a politician) in mind when he wrote this song, it was actually inspired by David Eisenhower, President Dwight D. Eisenhower's grandson. David Eisenhower happened to marry Richard Nixon's daughter, Julie.

Green Onions

Written by Al Jackson, Jr., Lewis Steinberg, Booker T. Jones and Steve Cropper

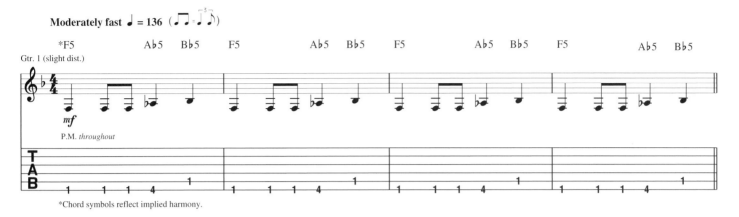

*Chord symbols reflect implied harmony.

Artist: Booker T. & The MG's **Album:** *Green Onions* **Year:** 1962 **Guitarist:** Steve Cropper	**Trivia:** This song came about when the band was waiting for Rockabilly singer Billy Lee Riley to arrive at his recording session (Booker T. & The MG's were the house band for Stax Records). Stax owner Jim Stewart recorded their jam and asked them to listen before they left the studio. When asked what the song title would be if it were released on record, Booker T. replied "'Green Onions,' because it's the nastiest thing I can think of and it's something you throw away." The song was a #3 hit.

Happy Together

Words and Music by Garry Bonner and Alan Gordon

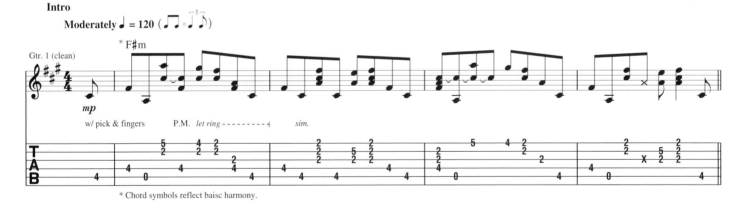

* Chord symbols reflect baisc harmony.

Artist: The Turtles **Album:** *Happy Together* **Year:** 1967 **Guitarists:** Al Nichol, Jim Tucker, Mark Volman	**Trivia:** Aided by numerous cover versions and appearances on movie soundtracks, performance rights organization BMI certified this #1 hit 8 million airplays in 2005, and also named it the 44th most-performed song of the 20th century.

Heart Full of Soul

Words and Music by Graham Gouldman

Track 10

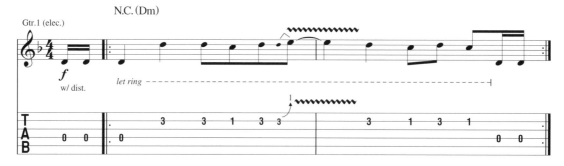

Artist: The Yardbirds **Album:** *Having a Rave Up* **Year:** 1965 **Guitarists:** Jeff Beck, Chris Dreja	**Trivia:** Since attempts at recording this song with a sitar part had failed, Jeff Beck emulated the instrument's sound on guitar.

Hey Bulldog

Words and Music by John Lennon and Paul McCartney

Track 11

Artist: The Beatles **Album:** *Yellow Submarine* **Year:** 1969 **Guitarists:** John Lennon, George Harrison	**Trivia:** This song's title was influenced by a moment in the recording session where Paul McCartney started barking without warning. Instead of singing the intended "hey bull-frog" he sang "hey bulldog."

I Can't Explain

Words and Music by Peter Townshend

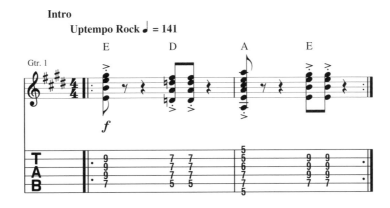

Artist: The Who

Album: none (released only as a single in the 1960s)

Year: 1965

Guitarist: Pete Townshend

Trivia: This song, in which Pete Townshend admits to copying the Kinks, has been covered by David Bowie and Scorpions, while portions of it have appeared in recordings by Elton John and the Clash.

Louie, Louie

Words and Music by Richard Berry

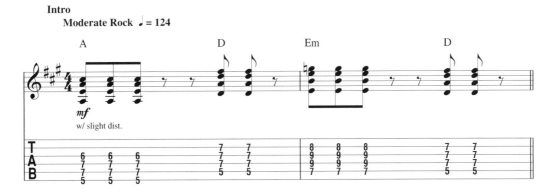

Artist: Kingsmen

Album: *The Kingsmen in Person*

Year: 1963

Guitarists: Jack Ely, Mike Mitchell

Trivia: The Kingsmen's version of this song sparked controversy in the 1960s, as parents across the country thought that the practically unintelligible lyrics must be profane. The FBI even conducted a 31-month investigation of the song, but concluded that they were "unable to interpret any of the wording in the record," so it was impossible to determine if the content was in violation of obscenity laws.

Nadine (Is It You)

Words and Music by Chuck Berry

Track 14

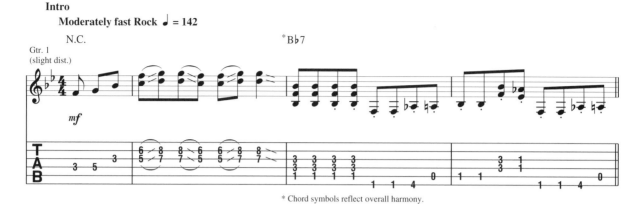

* Chord symbols reflect overall harmony.

Artist: Chuck Berry
Album: *Chuck Berry's Greatest Hits*
Year: 1964
Guitarist: Chuck Berry

Trivia: This is the first song Berry recorded after serving an 18-month sentence for violation of the Mann Act, which prohibits "white slavery" (forced prostitution) and transporting females across state lines for "immoral purposes." It is also the first of five Chuck Berry songs to hit the charts in 1964.

Not Fade Away

Words and Music by Charles Hardin and Norman Petty

Track 16

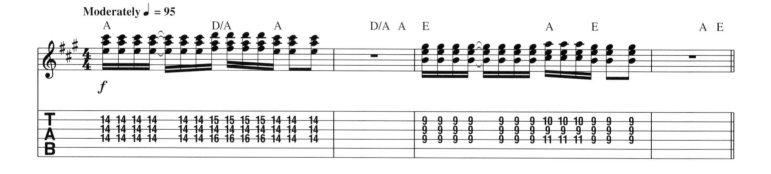

Artist: The Rolling Stones
Album: *England's Newest Hit Makers*
Year: 1964
Guitarists: Keith Richards, Brian Jones

Trivia: Besides the Stones version, this song has been recorded by the Grateful Dead and the Bobby Fuller Four, but it was actually the first single released by Rush in 1973. The B-side of this highly sought-after recording, called "You Can't Fight It," was the band's first original song.

No Particular Place to Go

Words and Music by Chuck Berry

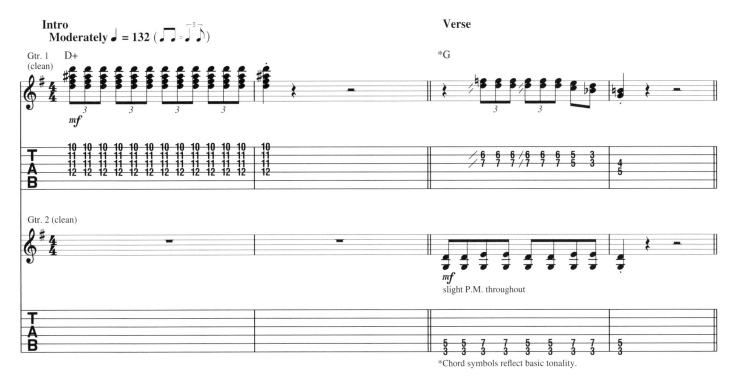

*Chord symbols reflect basic tonality.

Artist: Chuck Berry

Album: *St. Louis to Liverpool*

Year: 1964

Guitarists: Chuck Berry, Matt Murphy

Trivia: This song was the second and most successful single of Chuck Berry's post-jail comeback of 1964, peaking at #10 on the pop chart. It would be his last Top 10 hit for eight years.

Oh, Pretty Woman

Words and Music by Roy Orbison and Bill Dees

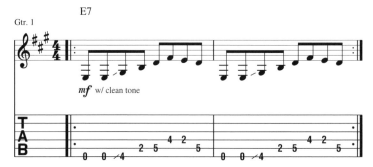

Artist: Roy Orbison

Album: *Orbisongs*

Year: 1965

Guitarists: Roy Orbison, Jerry Kennedy

Trivia: In 1989, controversial rap group 2 Live Crew sampled a portion of this song for a parody song called "Pretty Woman." The group's management requested a license from the song's publisher but was denied. However, 2 Live Crew recorded their parody anyway. The publisher sued for copyright infringement and unfair use, and the case was heard by the U.S. Supreme Court. The Court ruled in favor of 2 Live Crew, and stated that a for-profit parody may be protected under fair use law.

Paperback Writer

Words and Music by John Lennon and Paul McCartney

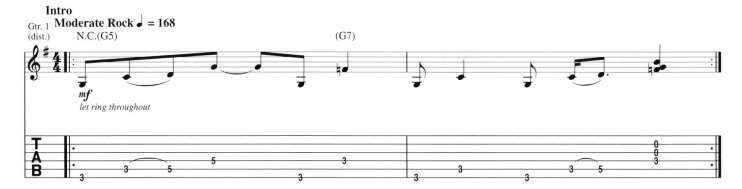

Artist: The Beatles

Album: none (released only as a single in the 1960s)

Year: 1966

Guitarists: John Lennon, George Harrison

Trivia: In the UK, the cover for this single depicted the band members with raw meat and decapitated baby dolls (commonly referred to as the "butcher cover"). This cover was too explicit to be released in the U.S., so live band member photos were used instead. This may not have been much of an improvement, as the photos of John Lennon and George Harrison are reversed so it appears as if they are playing left-handed.

Pipeline

By Bob Spickard and Brian Carman

Artist: The Chantays

Album: *Pipeline*

Year: 1963

Guitarists: Bob Spickard, Brian Carman

Trivia: Though this song was their only hit, a street has been named after this band: Chantays Boulevard is located next to Santa Ana High School in Southern California, where the original band members met.

(Ghost) Riders in the Sky
(A Cowboy Legend)

By Stan Jones

Intro
Bright Country Beat ♩ = 100

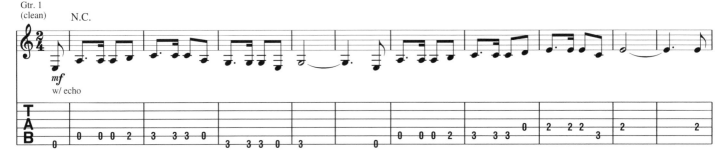

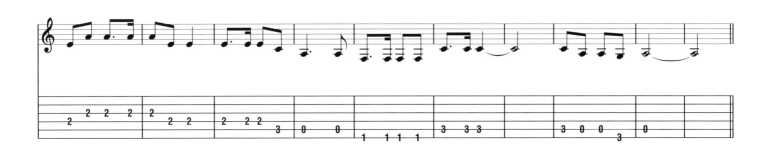

Artist: Ramrods

Album: none (released as a single)

Year: 1961

Guitarists: Vincent Bell Lee, Eugene Moore

Trivia: Not only are there dozens of recorded versions of this song, but there are also several versions of the Wild Hunt European folk myth, on which this song's lyrics appear to be based.

Runaway

Words and Music by Del Shannon and Max Crook

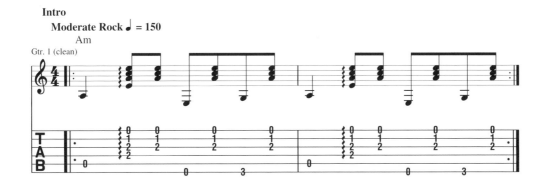

Artist: Del Shannon
Album: *Little Town Flirt*
Year: 1961
Guitarist: Del Shannon

Trivia: A few songs have paid homage to Del Shannon and this song: Tom Petty's "Running Down a Dream," "My Little Runaway" by the Stone Coyotes, and "When You Dream" by the Barenaked Ladies. Shannon even made an appearance as a police officer in the music video for Luis Cardenas's cover of the song in 1986.

Secret Agent Man

Words and Music by P.F. Sloan and Steve Barri

Artist: Johnny Rivers
Album: *Johnny Rivers' Golden Hits*
Year: 1966
Guitarist: Johnny Rivers

Trivia: Johnny Rivers's version of this song was the theme for the television show *Secret Agent*, and was also featured in the 1997 film *Austin Powers: International Man of Mystery*.

Substitute

Words and Music by Peter Townshend

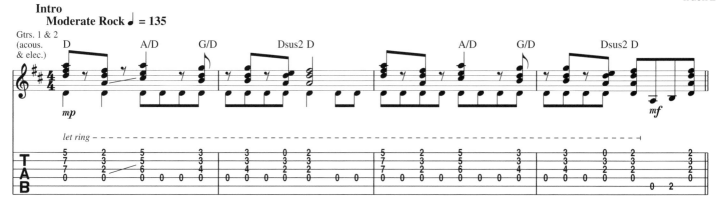

Artist: The Who **Album:** none (released only as a single in the 1960s) **Year:** 1966 **Guitarist:** Pete Townshend	**Trivia:** This song was The Who's first single since they broke ties with producer and manager Shel Talmy. As part of the settlement Talmy was paid a percentage of the royalties on each Who record for a period of five years.

Ticket to Ride

Words and Music by John Lennon and Paul McCartney

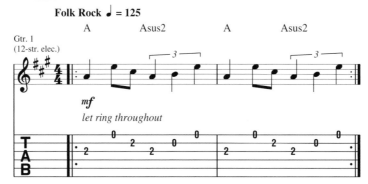

Artist: The Beatles **Album:** *Help!* **Year:** 1965 **Guitarists:** Paul McCartney, George Harrison	**Trivia:** This #1 hit marks the second time Paul McCartney played guitar parts on a Beatles record, the first being the song "Another Girl."

Walk Don't Run

By Johnny Smith

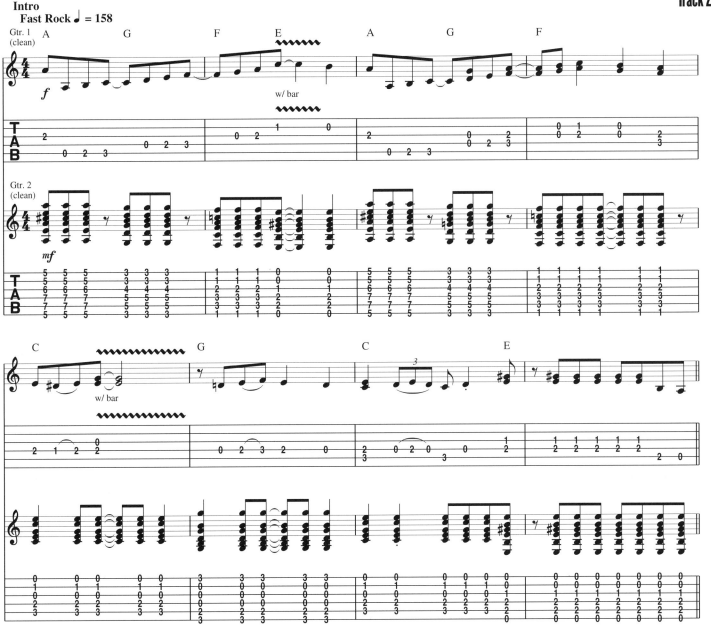

Artist: The Ventures

Album: *Walk Don't Run*

Year: 1960

Guitarists: Bob Bogle, Don Wilson

Trivia: The Ventures were the first band to hit the Top 10 with two versions of the same song: the original recording of "Walk Don't Run" peaked at #2 and "Walk Don't Run '64" reached #8.

We Gotta Get Out of This Place

Words and Music by Barry Mann and Cynthia Weil

Track 26

Artist: The Animals
Album: *Animal Tracks*
Year: 1965
Guitarist: Hilton Valentine

Trivia: Not only was this song adopted as an anthem by U.S. troops in the Vietnam War, it also appeared in Dennis Potter's television play *Stand Up, Nigel Barton*, the British television drama *Our Friends in the North*, and the 2004 film *Fahrenheit 9/11*.

White Room

Words and Music by Jack Bruce and Pete Brown

Track 27

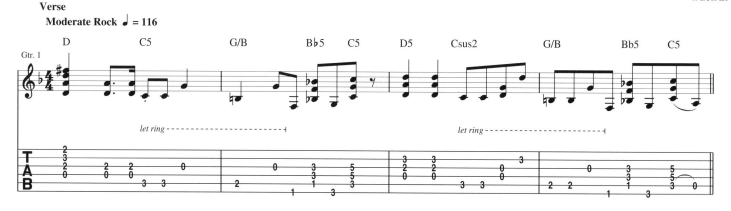

Artist: Cream
Album: *Wheels of Fire*
Year: 1968
Guitarist: Eric Clapton

Trivia: After Cream broke up, guitarist Eric Clapton refused to play this #6 hit live until 1985, when it was performed on *Late Night with David Letterman* and at Live Aid in Philadelphia.

Wild Thing

Words and Music by Chip Taylor

Track 28

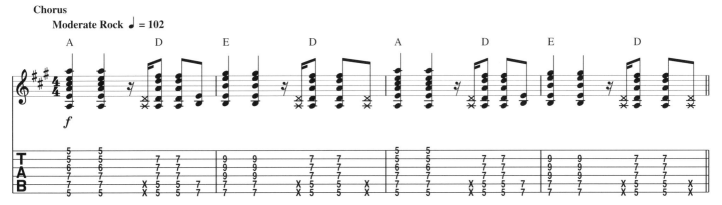

Artist: The Troggs	**Trivia:** This rock standard, written by actor Jon Voight's brother, was the only #1 single to be available on two different record labels simultaneously (due to a lack of communication between the band's management and British record label). *Billboard* combined the two releases into a single chart position even though they had different B-sides.
Album: *Wild Thing*	
Year: 1966	
Guitarist: Chris Britton	

You Shook Me

Written by Willie Dixon and J.B. Lenoir

Track 30

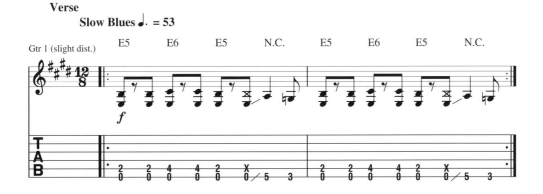

Artist: Led Zeppelin	**Trivia:** Co-writer Willie Dixon was properly credited for this song, along with "I Can't Quit You Baby," on Zeppelin's debut album, but he filed a lawsuit and was awarded damages for their use of portions of his songs "You Need Love" and "Bring It on Home" on *Led Zeppelin II*.
Album: *Led Zeppelin*	
Year: 1969	
Guitarist: Jimmy Page	

Windy

Words and Music by Ruthann Friedman

Track 29

Intro

Moderately ♩ = 133

N.C.

Gtr. 1 (clean)

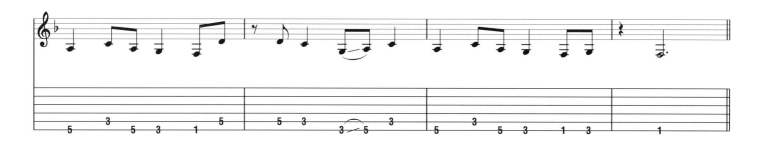

Artist: The Association

Album: *Insight Out*

Year: 1967

Guitarists: Russ Gigure, Jim Yester, Larry Ramos

Trivia: This song was a #1 hit for The Association, but it also became jazz guitarist Wes Montgomery's biggest *Billboard* Hot 100 hit peaking at #44.

Guitar Notation Legend

Guitar Music can be notated three different ways: on a *musical staff*, in *tablature*, and in *rhythm slashes*.

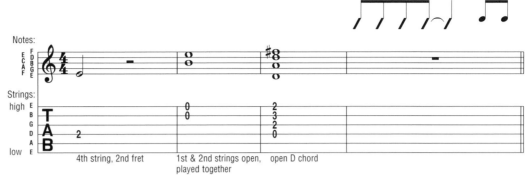

RHYTHM SLASHES are written above the staff. Strum chords in the rhythm indicated. Use the chord diagrams found at the top of the first page of the transcription for the appropriate chord voicings. Round noteheads indicate single notes.

THE MUSICAL STAFF shows pitches and rhythms and is divided by bar lines into measures. Pitches are named after the first seven letters of the alphabet.

TABLATURE graphically represents the guitar fingerboard. Each horizontal line represents a string, and each number represents a fret.

HALF-STEP BEND: Strike the note and bend up 1/2 step.

WHOLE-STEP BEND: Strike the note and bend up one step.

GRACE NOTE BEND: Strike the note and immediately bend up as indicated.

SLIGHT (MICROTONE) BEND: Strike the note and bend up 1/4 step.

BEND AND RELEASE: Strike the note and bend up as indicated, then release back to the original note. Only the first note is struck.

PRE-BEND: Bend the note as indicated, then strike it.

VIBRATO: The string is vibrated by rapidly bending and releasing the note with the fretting hand.

WIDE VIBRATO: The pitch is varied to a greater degree by vibrating with the fretting hand.

HAMMER-ON: Strike the first (lower) note with one finger, then sound the higher note (on the same string) with another finger by fretting it without picking.

PULL-OFF: Place both fingers on the notes to be sounded. Strike the first note and without picking, pull the finger off to sound the second (lower) note.

LEGATO SLIDE: Strike the first note and then slide the same fret-hand finger up or down to the second note. The second note is not struck.

SHIFT SLIDE: Same as legato slide, except the second note is struck.

TRILL: Very rapidly alternate between the notes indicated by continuously hammering on and pulling off.

TAPPING: Hammer ("tap") the fret indicated with the pick-hand index or middle finger and pull off to the note fretted by the fret hand.

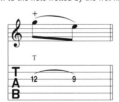

NATURAL HARMONIC: Strike the note while the fret-hand lightly touches the string directly over the fret indicated.

PINCH HARMONIC: The note is fretted normally and a harmonic is produced by adding the edge of the thumb or the tip of the index finger of the pick hand to the normal pick attack.

PICK SCRAPE: The edge of the pick is rubbed down (or up) the string, producing a scratchy sound.

MUFFLED STRINGS: A percussive sound is produced by laying the fret hand across the string(s) without depressing, and striking them with the pick hand.

PALM MUTING: The note is partially muted by the pick hand lightly touching the string(s) just before the bridge.

RAKE: Drag the pick across the strings indicated with a single motion.

TREMOLO PICKING: The note is picked as rapidly and continuously as possible.

VIBRATO BAR DIVE AND RETURN: The pitch of the note or chord is dropped a specified number of steps (in rhythm) then returned to the original pitch.

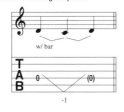

VIBRATO BAR SCOOP: Depress the bar just before striking the note, then quickly release the bar.

VIBRATO BAR DIP: Strike the note and then immediately drop a specified number of steps, then release back to the original pitch.

RECORDED VERSIONS®
The Best Note-For-Note Transcriptions Available

ALL BOOKS INCLUDE TABLATURE

00692015	Aerosmith – Greatest Hits $22.95
00690603	Aerosmith – O Yeah! (Ultimate Hits) $24.95
00690178	Alice in Chains – Acoustic $19.95
00694865	Alice in Chains – Dirt $19.95
00690387	Alice in Chains – Nothing Safe:
	The Best of the Box $19.95
00690812	All American Rejects – Move Along $19.95
00694932	Allman Brothers Band – Volume 1 . . . . . .$24.95
00694933	Allman Brothers Band – Volume 2 . . . . . .$24.95
00694934	Allman Brothers Band – Volume 3 . . . . . .$24.95
00690755	Alter Bridge – One Day Remains $19.95
00690609	Audioslave $19.95
00690804	Audioslave – Out of Exile $19.95
00690366	Bad Company – Original Anthology, Book 1 . . .$19.95
00690503	Beach Boys – Very Best of $19.95
00690489	Beatles – 1 . . . .$24.95
00694929	Beatles – 1962-1966 . . . .$24.95
00694930	Beatles – 1967-1970 . . . .$24.95
00694832	Beatles – For Acoustic Guitar $22.95
00690110	Beatles – White Album (Book 1) $19.95
00690792	Beck – Guero $19.95
00692385	Berry, Chuck $19.95
00692200	Black Sabbath –
	We Sold Our Soul for Rock 'N' Roll $19.95
00690674	Blink-182 . . . .$19.95
00690389	Blink-182 – Enema of the State $19.95
00690523	Blink-182 – Take Off Your Pants & Jacket . .$19.95
00690491	Bowie, David – Best of $19.95
00690764	Breaking Benjamin – We Are Not Alone . .$19.95
00690451	Buckley, Jeff – Collection $24.95
00690590	Clapton, Eric – Anthology $29.95
00690415	Clapton Chronicles – Best of Eric Clapton . .$18.95
00690074	Clapton, Eric – The Cream of Clapton $24.95
00690716	Clapton, Eric – Me and Mr. Johnson $19.95
00694869	Clapton, Eric – Unplugged $22.95
00690162	Clash – Best of The $19.95
00690593	Coldplay – A Rush of Blood to the Head . .$19.95
00690806	Coldplay – X & Y $19.95
00694940	Counting Crows – August & Everything After . .$19.95
00690401	Creed – Human Clay $19.95
00690352	Creed – My Own Prison $19.95
00690551	Creed – Weathered $19.95
00690648	Croce, Jim – Very Best of $19.95
00690572	Cropper, Steve – Soul Man $19.95
00690613	Crosby, Stills & Nash – Best of $19.95
00690777	Crossfade $19.95
00690289	Deep Purple – Best of $17.95
00690347	Doors, The – Anthology $22.95
00690348	Doors, The – Essential Guitar Collection . .$16.95
00690810	Fall Out Boy – From Under the Cork Tree . .$19.95
00690664	Fleetwood Mac – Best of $19.95
00690808	Foo Fighters – In Your Honor $19.95
00694920	Free – Best of $19.95
00690773	Good Charlotte –
	The Chronicles of Life and Death $19.95
00690601	Good Charlotte –
	The Young and the Hopeless $19.95
00690697	Hall, Jim – Best of $19.95
00694798	Harrison, George – Anthology $19.95
00690778	Hawk Nelson – Letters to the President . .$19.95
00692930	Hendrix, Jimi – Are You Experienced? . . .$24.95
00692931	Hendrix, Jimi – Axis: Bold As Love $22.95
00690608	Hendrix, Jimi – Blue Wild Angel $24.95
00692932	Hendrix, Jimi – Electric Ladyland $24.95
00690017	Hendrix, Jimi – Live at Woodstock $24.95

00690602	Hendrix, Jimi – Smash Hits $19.95
00690692	Idol, Billy – Very Best of $19.95
00690688	Incubus – A Crow Left of the Murder $19.95
00690457	Incubus – Make Yourself $19.95
00690544	Incubus – Morningview $19.95
00690730	Jackson, Alan – Guitar Collection $19.95
00690721	Jet – Get Born $19.95
00690684	Jethro Tull – Aqualung $19.95
00690647	Jewel – Best of $19.95
00690751	John5 – Vertigo $19.95
00690271	Johnson, Robert – New Transcriptions . . .$24.95
00699131	Joplin, Janis – Best of $19.95
00690427	Judas Priest – Best of $19.95
00690742	Killers, The – Hot Fuss $19.95
00694903	Kiss – Best of $24.95
00690780	Korn – Greatest Hits, Volume 1 . . . .$22.95
00690726	Lavigne, Avril – Under My Skin $19.95
00690679	Lennon, John – Guitar Collection $19.95
00690785	Limp Bizkit – Best of $19.95
00690781	Linkin Park – Hybrid Theory $22.95
00690782	Linkin Park – Meteora $22.95
00690783	Live, Best of $19.95
00690743	Los Lonely Boys $19.95
00690720	Lostprophets – Start Something $19.95
00694954	Lynyrd Skynyrd – New Best of $19.95
00690577	Malmsteen, Yngwie – Anthology $24.95
00690754	Manson, Marilyn – Lest We Forget $19.95
00694956	Marley, Bob – Legend $19.95
00694945	Marley, Bob – Songs of Freedom $24.95
00690748	Maroon5 – 1.22.03 Acoustic $19.95
00690657	Maroon5 – Songs About Jane $19.95
00120080	McLean, Don – Songbook $19.95
00694951	Megadeth – Rust in Peace $22.95
00690768	Megadeth – The System Has Failed $19.95
00690505	Mellencamp, John – Guitar Collection $19.95
00690646	Metheny, Pat – One Quiet Night $19.95
00690565	Metheny, Pat – Rejoicing $19.95
00690558	Metheny, Pat – Trio: 99>00 . . . .$19.95
00690561	Metheny, Pat – Trio > Live $22.95
00690040	Miller, Steve, Band – Young Hearts $19.95
00690769	Modest Mouse – Good News
	for People Who Love Bad News $19.95
00690786	Mudvayne – The End of All Things to Come . .$22.95
00690787	Mudvayne – L.D. 50 . . . .$22.95
00690794	Mudvayne – Lost and Found $19.95
00690611	Nirvana $22.95
00694883	Nirvana – Nevermind $19.95
00690026	Nirvana – Unplugged in New York $19.95
00690739	No Doubt – Rock Steady $22.95
00690807	Offspring, The – Greatest Hits $19.95
00694847	Osbourne, Ozzy – Best of $22.95
00690399	Osbourne, Ozzy – Ozzman Cometh $19.95
00694855	Pearl Jam – Ten $19.95
00690439	Perfect Circle, A – Mer De Noms $19.95
00690661	Perfect Circle, A – Thirteenth Step $19.95
00690499	Petty, Tom – Definitive Guitar Collection . .$19.95
00690731	Pillar – Where Do We Go from Here? $19.95
00690428	Pink Floyd – Dark Side of the Moon $19.95
00693864	Police, The – Best of $19.95
00694975	Queen – Greatest Hits $24.95
00690670	Queensryche – Very Best of $19.95
00694910	Rage Against the Machine $19.95
00690055	Red Hot Chili Peppers –
	Bloodsugarsexmagik $19.95
00690584	Red Hot Chili Peppers – By the Way $19.95

00690379	Red Hot Chili Peppers – Californication . .$19.9
00690673	Red Hot Chili Peppers – Greatest Hits $19.9
00690511	Reinhardt, Django – Definitive Collection . .$19.9
00690779	Relient K – MMHMM $19.9
00690643	Relient K – Two Lefts Don't
	Make a Right...But Three Do $19.9
00690631	Rolling Stones – Guitar Anthology $24.9
00690685	Roth, David Lee – Eat 'Em and Smile $19.9
00690694	Roth, David Lee – Guitar Anthology $24.9
00690749	Saliva – Survival of the Sickest $19.9
00690031	Santana's Greatest Hits $19.9
00690796	Schenker, Michael – Very Best of $19.9
00690566	Scorpions – Best of $19.9
00690604	Seger, Bob – Guitar Collection $19.9
00690530	Slipknot – Iowa $19.9
00690733	Slipknot – Vol. 3 (The Subliminal Verses) . .$19.9
00690691	Smashing Pumpkins Anthology $19.9
00120004	Steely Dan – Best of $24.9
00694921	Steppenwolf – Best of $22.9
00690655	Stern, Mike – Best of $19.9
00690689	Story of the Year – Page Avenue $19.9
00690520	Styx Guitar Collection $19.9
00120081	Sublime $19.9
00690519	SUM 41 – All Killer No Filler $19.9
00690771	SUM 41 – Chuck $19.9
00690767	Switchfoot – The Beautiful Letdown $19.9
00690815	Switchfoot – Nothing Is Sound $19.9
00690799	System of a Down – Mezmerize $19.9
00690531	System of a Down – Toxicity $19.9
00694824	Taylor, James – Best of $16.9
00690737	3 Doors Down – The Better Life $22.9
00690776	3 Doors Down – Seventeen Days $19.9
00690683	Trower, Robin – Bridge of Sighs $19.9
00690740	Twain, Shania – Guitar Collection $19.9
00699191	U2 – Best of: 1980-1990 . . . .$19.9
00690732	U2 – Best of: 1990-2000 . . . .$19.9
00690775	U2 – How to Dismantle an Atomic Bomb . .$22.9
00694411	U2 – The Joshua Tree $19.9
00660137	Vai, Steve – Passion & Warfare $24.9
00690370	Vaughan, Stevie Ray and Double Trouble –
	The Real Deal: Greatest Hits Volume 2 . .$22.9
00690116	Vaughan, Stevie Ray – Guitar Collection . .$24.9
00660058	Vaughan, Stevie Ray –
	Lightnin' Blues 1983-1987 . . . .$24.9
00694835	Vaughan, Stevie Ray – The Sky Is Crying . .$22.9
00690015	Vaughan, Stevie Ray – Texas Flood $19.9
00690772	Velvet Revolver – Contraband $22.9
00690071	Weezer (The Blue Album) $19.9
00690800	Weezer – Make Believe $19.9
00690447	Who, The – Best of $24.9
00690672	Williams, Dar – Best of $19.9
00690710	Yellowcard – Ocean Avenue $19.9
00690589	ZZ Top Guitar Anthology $22.9